# Notice: All Non-Employees Should Wash Their Hands

An Oddity Potpourri Outlook Poetry Book

by

Samantha Grace Mesman

Illustrations by Alexis Lee

**DORRANCE**
PUBLISHING CO
EST. 1920
PITTSBURGH, PENNSYLVANIA 15238

Dorrance Publishing Co
585 Alpha Drive
Suite 103
Pittsburgh, PA 15238
Visit our website at *www.dorrancebookstore.com*

ISBN: 978-1-6366-1203-4
eISBN: 978-1-6366-1793-0

Dedicated to my best friend, Eric.

Dear Reader,

Notice that to the left of the poems include backstories, quotes or more short poems to "warm up" your poetry muscles, thus preventing any related injury or strains. As always, your best interest was kept in mind.

With much consideration,
Samantha Mesman

Who else is tired of small talk? Your silent pause to ponder that question is agreement enough. This is for people who want more from conversations. We're talking more depth, more connections, and more feelings. The other person likely wants to approach too but if we wait around for the right moment then you may have to wait forever. That's why YOU must make the moment. Let's step out of our comfort zone and be the first to initiate some quality jibber-jabber. Behold, this cringey "Awk-word" poem as it highlights debilitating effects caused by shyness.

# Awk-word

This time I'll open my mouth.
Searching for words, the right ones, to come perfectly out.
Hello again, Fear, perchance any Confidence remains in here.
Step forward if so, and by all means, please make yourself known.
Introductions, judgments, apprehension and questions.
Speaking of such, may I have your complete and utter attention?
Standing up still face to face,
Facing expectant eyes as an audience awaits.
My mind brims full of blanks spills over into nothingness,
All previous thoughts vacate been plumb erased.

With whom I share a pleasure to speak?
Perhaps we previously passed alongside some silly street,
Into the self, comforted by thoughts and doubts where I quietly keep.
One on one we stroll on by,
Toothless smile, averted eyes,
How pathetic am I?
An impossible feat to squawk out one measly "Hi."
Gut clenching, breath catching,
Throat clearing, phlegm phlegmy,
Pleased to meet you, call me Sammie.

After eons into the evolution,
Considering ourselves civilized humans.
What once a prehistoric solution,
Now present-day debilitating courage reducing,
Mechanism. That's not social, passively coasting,
Not really living life to the most and
Too wrapped up in our own heads,
Can we step out of this comfort land?

Pleasantly glad that you are listening,
For everyone wants a way to be heard.
These tactics, though rather absurd,
Highlight my demeanor being highly Awkward.
Here we'll use plenty of practical playful words,
Pinky promise it will tickle a chuckle, and spark a little spark,
Inspire your own voice, your own beat,
Illuminating that brilliantly bright heart,

This here is a good place to start.

This collection is nothing if not personal. Although we find ourselves rooted only one poem deep into this book, the metaphorical clock strikes at "high time" to clear the air with my dirty laundry. I truly feel safe in confiding this intimate information because you do not know my face, only my words. Wait, did you just look at the back cover? ...Why, you little!

In all honesty, who hasn't been a hoe? It's a phase of life, a rite of passage... or an excuse to be "ratchet." For the record, I am not a hoe... well, anymore. Sorry, Dad.

# Tragic Ass

Question: How to make the booty grow minus those quads too?
Answer: no idea.
Stick a seed, see it be, sprout it... Ch-Ch-Ch-Chia!

Chia-Pet this booty with your eyes but venture no further,
Take a seat. Hands off, please!
Do you think this is a charity?
First, realize you got to buy me expensive coffee or exotic tea.
Time ain't free. I'll smile, I'll fake sweet,
Never no, just agree.

Boy, let's lie together,
That's it, nod and agree,
Pretend that your interests are piquing with me.
Later we can lye together,
The known is you're present for that one fucking thing.

That thing be to fuck.
Verb. Word. Verbatim which is key.
Presently, tell me I'm pretty.
Tell me, tell me.
Feed me. Feed my ego.
Go. Grow.
That's it, I'm happy.
Oh, finally, momentarily content with the way that things be.

High time to pitch a tent.
Let's do this shit, make it quick,
The sooner we get it over with
All but one mistake,
I'll never learn from.
Oops.

One sheep, two sheep, three sheep, four. One little sheep suffers anxiety and is unable to sleep ever more. Looks out yonder barn window, wishing on the brightest star, to fall deeply into a comatose state so all may compensate for many nights lost.

That little sheep is me.

# Insomniac's Almanac

Last night, I couldn't sleep. Laid awake the whole time with my racing mind.
Staring up at the ceiling. My head loops thoughts around on repeat.
Imagining a reality where I actually say what I mean.
No more Mr. Nice... I mean, *grabs boob* (*They're still there*) Mrs. Nice me.
Comebacks come so, so easily. *Like ha! Take that!*
This is what I'd do if it happened differently.

Wait, what's happening? *Oh, girl, try to fall asleep.*
Focus hard, simply breathe. Though not too hard,
Count one hundred soft fluffy sheep.
Finally, relaxed. *Deep breath*
Nope. Feeling a spazzy spasm urge to pee. Why is this such a problem for me?
My bladder's aged just over 23.
Excuse me, Dear Santa, next Christmas 2020,
Only one thing of dire need, like a fresh pair of healthy kidneys.
Promise to be good, please, oh pretty please!

Checking out the clock, counting down the hours left for me...
Six hours until daylight.
Five, well, that's a good chunk.
Three, Hm—decent nap.
One, next day gonna suck.
Must be my last resort to turn to obviously.
Because nothing really works except the caffeine.
*Hey barista, hey-hey barista!*
Pour me eight shots, eight shots each for,
Each for the hour of sleep that was lost,
You say, "No more!" Then you cut me off, "*Oh, what the fu——.*"

This really hurts because my heavy eyes hold 50-pound weights.
Dark circles underneath: no shades. Sure, you could say, "I stayed up late."

Attention impaired very hard to think straight.

Why is everyone staring at me? Did I just become the next celebrity?

My mood goes back and forth a-swinging!

One moment there's laughing, next some crying, for no reason.

Although, puppies outside are playing in the leaves.

Who knew it could do such a number on me?

Right around the corner, just around the corner,

Insomnia transforms into euphoria.

As life becomes a walking living dream

Won't you come and sleepwalk with me?

Life is but a walking living dream

Won't you come and sleepwalk…

with me?

*Meditation molds magic moments. That's a lofty alliteration. However, through conscious rest and through conscious breath we can access this internal universe of unconditional love, peace, and bliss. Were you aware you have been breathing this whole time? It's simple, yet easy to forget. You are alive, dear Reader! ALIVE! Life can't be so bad if you're still breathing.*

# Cosmos and Effects

So vast and so mighty,
Source from the sky,
Shoots sunbeams into beings,
In this vessel to exist, to occupy. *But why?*

To learn and experience, fail as well rise,
Feeling every emotion, now truly alive.
Though simply human, spirit bound to us all.
Flora, fauna, both equally big and small.
Merely one of many, home be our earth.
Endless wonder considered in this beautiful universe.

Do what you love, for each precious life,
Has passion, has a destiny and flows down paths meant to be.
Don't resist. Let go and let carry.

Strive for intention!
Question these old conventions.
To think slowly for a second finds your own explanation.
Interwoven network of connections.
*Psst! It's a matrix.* What's a matrix?
*Pull out your brain from your pants and Google that shit!*

Comprised of a million, billion or infinite,
Choices, choices,
Changing fates, changing courses.
Seems scary, doesn't it?
I see it thrilling, all depends on how you look at it.

Who am I?
Little white girl acting like,

I got this special secret look, this insight.
Like something speaking through me,
Don't claim to be a Messiah.
Freely feeling on my newly opened third eye.
This rap is long enough,
And I'm tired of my rhymes,
'Bout time to say goodbye!

You do your life,
I do mine.

These are a few of my favorite things:

A soft, fuzzy bathrobe
A juicy hardcover rom-com
A reasonably timed bedtime

Yes, I am 25 years old. And yes, I am describing an ideal Friday night. Let's boogie on down to sleep-town!

# Original-Grandma

I'm a Grandma, I wear my pants up high.
Tuck in my sweater because I get chilled at night.
Don't like to stay up late, bedtime sharply at 9:00.
Sleep is la crème de la crème, best part of being alive.
*What would an OG do if she doesn't sleep?*
OGs like to read! Relish in the books.
Remember those "things with the pages" since screens hurt my eyes.

Cruising down Main, roll up to the coffee shop,
Drink order placed: Not too cold or too hot.
*I spy with my little cataract,* the homies in the back,
'Sup Albert, Amos, they'll wave to me "Hi."
Certainly, you're not surprised... all of them are aged over 65.
Wishing to stay forever although time isn't on my side.
We exchange physical addresses...
Promise to them I'll write.

Break it down low,
Like fuzzy bathrobe.
Fuzzy bathrobe,
and slippers!
Fuzzy bathrobe.
Fuzzy bathrobe,
and slippers!

On a real note, I do have friends.
We are chilling at the park before it gets dark.

I feed them... bread.

I'm talking about those motherfucking fucking ducks at Randall Park, BITCH.

Getting lost in the moment is a wonderful, freeing feeling. When one finds time to let go of time then it is time well spent.

# It's Poetry Time

The good speeds too quickly by,
While the hard drags down, forgetting to fly.
Fastened around the wrist, body ornament,
Crystals to adorn, compliments adoring it.
A statement is how it's worn.
Designer names showcased but all the same.
5:01 is 5:01.
Unless rechecked again, now 5:02.
Does a difference of one single minute really matter to you?
*Wait a minute!* Two past five? Where's my tequila sunrise?

Frustration when late, impatience if early,
On-time perfection, rarely occurring.
All eyes watch the clock, sound the buzzing,
Bodies rise and march to rhythms of honking, speeding, cursing.
Poor humans enslaved to the alarm.

The palate of time passed enjoys flavors bittersweet.
Memories are savored, moments such as these,
Truly a trick of the psyche.
For when we find ourselves living in this longing,
A venture back we are wanting,
To change something, one thing said.
Over and over, tumbling in head.
That happened back there, that's not here.

Nor shall we fret of what lies ahead.
There is no rush, do not hurry.
Things will happen when they must.
For fear far beyond is futile, pointless use to worry.
The future neither exists here.

We know so much, except what is left, left for us.
Each day gone equals one day less.
That knowledge, our guess, is as good as it gets.
Remember, Life is limitless.
Time for this life may be limited.
Lifetimes countless, time to count on this as the countdown persists.
Being present in each moment is a gift so cherish it.

They say we have one life to live, calling complete BS.
*Hello?* This is not goodbye. No.
I'll wave back to you next as a beautiful butterfly.

This is the woman I aspire to be. She's a free spirit who decides to shave her head because she wants to. What a badass. What a gal.

# Fish-town Hippie

Fish-town Hippie,
Carelessly,
Walking backwards,
Whistling.
To a tune that makes her heart sing.
Now a soft, salty breeze,
Rolls in gently.

Well, the breeze would have rustled her hair,
If it were really there.
Removed without a care,
Due to her consciously,
Ignoring to obey society.
Defining her own beauty.
It was her choice, you see.
She's one of the few that's free.

Fish-town Hippie, I envy.
What a colorful life,
Writing your own melody.

Talking to strangers,
Absence of danger,
More love and less anger,
Must be no feeling greater.
Release these insecurities.

Why can't we be?
More like Fish-town Hippie,
With soul shining.
Wishing my outsides reflected my insides but,

I got a secret, in us her spirit,
Ever so brightly,
Gleaming.

*My wintertime cardio regimen consists of a precarious jog from the car to the house or vice versa. A girl's gotta move but carefully as humanly-girlishly possible. Besides that, winter becomes a sedentary game called "hurry up and wait" until we roll into summer. Why, why such caution heeded? Well, nosey Reader, if you must know, I don't have health insurance and to keep these ol' hips intact is quite delightful.*

*Q: Why is Yakima, WA, dubbed thee "Palm Springs of Washington"?*

*A: Yet another marvelous question, "oh wise and curious one." As I wish there was an adequately marvelous answer to match such a question.*

# It's Fucking Cold Outside

Look out for the ice on the road!
Cars swerve off to work they go,
Crashing, crunching, smashing, smunching,
Bumper tails reared up high getting towed,
The pretty women notice down the tips of their nose,
Tippy-toes tap gas pedals,
Around steering wheels white knuckles enclose.
Inch by inch, sour faces tightly pinched,
Lovely leery ladies drive real, real slow.

*Oh, feeling happy!*
Sucks to be you but at least it isn't me!
For all I care is getting there in one piece.
My lack of empathy generosity,
Extends to only mild-moderate pity.
HA-HA-HO-HO-HE.

*Oh, Shit!* **\*Slam on brakes\*** *This can't be happening to me.*
Narrator lost an advantage from her vantage point. *Ouch!*
Ego lands hard on its butt joint. *Bleeping Bleep!!!*
Censored foul words fly away followed by exclamation points.
Fourth wall broken trick. This hypocrite throws one big fat fit.
Who mostly, closely dodged a near-miss hit.
*(Well, enough about me. Now, back to my story.)*

Manly men drive double XL trucks,
Hoping to beef up their luck.
*We all know what that means...* Come out and come clean,
Can you say...Compensating?
*Compensating!*

*Newsflash:* The frigid cold doesn't help anything. Not to mention that little disadvantage already.

Oh, you'll never find me in states resembling Wyoming.
But what the yuck, that lying sign reads,

*Welcome to Yakima, Washington's "Palm Springs"*?!

Some twisted joke that just isn't funny.
'Cause it's fucking cold outside.

*So don't go outside!*

*Now presenting... Tinder, The Musical! Look out, folks! As the millennial dating scene meets Broadway in this fresh, pathetically realistic tale of two screen-crossed lovers. Where one average Joe schmuck tries out his luck on a pretty lame duck. Don't forget the breadsticks! Coming soon to a theatre near you...*

# Tinder, The Musical!

Shucks, it's nice to meet you.

My name is Ashley. I just like to have fun!

So, if you treat me right,

Take me out to *Olive Garden* tonight,

Then I'll let you stick it in my bum.


My bum diddly bumptious bum bum.


The price sure seems right,

Soup and salad would be nice.

$9.99!

It's a luck of a deal, really quite a tuck of a deal.

Oh, what a steal and only for a feel ;)

Upgrading the night to a full meal,

Boy, don't you dare forget...

The bottomless breadsticks.


Heigh-ho, heigh-ho, it's back to your place we'll go!

To play pretend like a show,

Pretense foreplay nice and slow.

Buttery dripping, breadstick dipping, Italian kitchen cooking show.

No pressure, you be Chef Sous.

High expectations to be tossed good,

Or else it will sound like WWII Gobbledygook.

Nein Nein NEIN!


'Sup.

The name's Chad.

I got the body like a Dad.

Hey-hoe, hey-hoe, if you text me back,

I pinky promise that I'll last...

Long as I can!

Come on, let's be real, soup and salad is the deal.

At the very least, enjoy a free, "please-go-out-with-me" meal.

Girl, I won't forget,

Those bottomless breadsticks.


Chad: "Hey Siri, what does 'Nein, Nein, Nein' mean? Asking for a friend."

Having a period sucks. Having a kid would suck more. The universe has a twisted sense of humor and uteruses do too. My menses took pleasure in the fact of arriving one day after the negative pregnancy test. How convenient.

If only a uterus could speak, then what would it say?

# Peeking Period Pains

Lo and behold,
The marvelous feminine flow.
Hint hint: Down below.
No, never gross.
Monthly supposedly physiologically supposed.
Dull aching sensations, panty-staining confessions,
Sharp zinging pains, twing and twang.
A sassiness in the uterus yearns to come out.
*Holy cramp!*
Silly volatile words slip from her smartass mouth.
Easy fix.
Shove down sour candies and bitter dark chocolates,
Sweetens up the harsh dialogue... *a bit.*

Combining all crimson colors of the hemorrhagic rainbow.
Magenta, fuchsia, and scarlet,
Swirl and twirl together,
Neatly wrap up in a sanguine bow.
A fabulous feminine monthly gift.
Thank Heavens I don't have a kid.
*Yippee!* Marks *another four weeks pregnancy free.*

PS: Ladies, if smells smell smelly,
Be it foul or display colors tinged green...
Wait not Tanner stage 5 and please get that seen.

This is your body so rejoice, everybody,
Nature is happening.

*Juicy, juicy moments when the dream's so sweet and feels so real. As the hazy sleep-fog lifts then so do those ripe dreams drift, farther and farther away. If only we could hold on tightly to dreams and reel them back into our possession. Like holding onto a slippery wet fish because no matter how massive the effort, inevitably, the fishy slips out through our fingers. Hence the slippery wetness of the fish. Alas, a dream must be released into the metaphorical sea, finally freed.*

**WARNING: DO NOT TRY THIS
WHIMSICAL METAPHOR AT HOME.
(no actual fish were harmed in the making.)**

# Liquid Dreams

Dawn begins its breaking,
As the day is waking,
While dreams slip,
Slip away.
Desperate to remember scenes,
Leaking out of fickle memory.
When we forget, where does it go?
Disappears into thin air,
Left feeling loss and despair.
Letting go is the effortless struggle.
Maybe dreams come back,
If they are meant to be.

*I told you not to forget them! They're back by popular demand! Gluten has made its not-so-silent comeback. Ancient proverbs reveal, "A rich man consumes countless breadsticks while a poor man snacks on snacks gluten-free."*

*Stoics had it right all along.*

*\*Sources have not been cited.*

# Breadsticks Bromance

*Ladies and Chads, bread roll, please!*

We are here to celebrate at the restaurant.
Sit down, open up menus, *"Yeah, what do you want?"*

Then before you know, the waiter walks over; pitter-patter,
Steam sensually rises softly from his big ol' platter.
An abrupt silence hushes down our chitter-chatter.
Our mouths begin to water,
Over the...warm fluffy bread!
Dip you in oil or vinegar.
We fill up on you before the appetizer.
Beauty brightly blinding so go grab your visor.
Saliva flowing freely like *Old Faithful* geyser.
Warm fluffy bread, my sweetest comfort, much better than dessert.

The waiter starts to talk about the specials tonight,
Honestly, I don't really care. I DON'T CARE.
Do I dare... ask for more? Impossible.
Drool dripping on the floor, language garbled: unintelligible.
Visions of heavenly sliced dough danced in my head.
*Oh, please* bring more fluffy bread. *Ah-hem*, I said, "PLEASE BRING MORE
FLUFFY BREAD!"
...
Sincerest apologies to the waiter. Our minds are not made up yet on the order.
This low-key gluten hoarder, needs more time to think but another loaf will
do,
Going in round two... people say there's always room.
*(In a random extra-designated dessert stomach.)*
Yet mine is dedicated to...more warm fluffy bread.

Chad: "Uh, what do you think, Abby—I mean **\*cough-cough\*** Ashley. What do you want to drink?"

*Meanwhile, the waiter now on edge, expectantly watches and waits. Eyes darting back and forth between the customer's face. Patience dwindling. Tolerance diminishing. Pushing him closer and closer to the brink. What, oh, what will they drink??*

Ashley: "Uhm, I'd like—"

Chad: "Yeah, we'll stick to water. We're cheap bastards, chewing on free bread."

Enough is enough. And enough has been said. What more is there to add?

Only but one measly loaf of,

Heavenly, crispy, soft, gooey, buttery, flaky, and *(don't forget)* cakey,

Bread.

What sucks about life? Many things do but to name a few:
The beginning of a workweek
The start of school
and diets (in general) all suck.

Though what do these suckers have in common? Think, think, think! They typically fall on a Monday. Ah-ha! The culprit has revealed itself. My solution is simply obvious yet obviously simple.
The Proposal: We get rid of all the Mondays then ALL our problems will be solved. (At least those three mentioned above.)

Shall we celebrate this revelation with some cake, anyone?
Yes! Let them eat cake (as Marie once said) since we've mysteriously run out of bread.

# There Once Was A Day Called Monday

Say bye-bye to Mondays, they're not really fun days!
Not as sweet as Sundays *(more of a sugar-free substitute taste.)*
Wave bye-bye to Mondays, worries are quickly carried away,
So the world will be a better place.

Take a moment to listen as I go out on a limb and,
Offer to make Mondays illegal as a bad word,
Officially: never spoken again, never heard.
Sounds simple.

First, cross it off in our calendars, erasing another naughty word forever.
Rid it from vocabulary, consequently white-out in all dictionaries.
Any further mention of Mon—*Shh!* Is completely fictionary, fable, remove it
from the table.
Not enough? Easy-peasey greater lengths if need be.
How about mandatory Monday vasectomies? Hence, they no longer breed.

What about the remaining Mondays?
Let us brainstorm ideas on the fly,
How about we bomb them, BOMB THEM! And rip out their insides—*(Okay,
you get the point.)*

Say bye-bye to Mondays, they're not really fun days!
Not as sweet as Sundays *(more of a sugar-free substitute taste).*
Wave bye-bye to Mondays, worries are quickly carried away,
So the world will be a better place.

All the good habits that you want to make,
All the bad ones that you try to break,
Never turn out anyways, it's all work but no play!
Because what happens on a Monday tends to stay on a Monday...

Like diets.

Admittedly, no mention for my question when people have the best intention.
Advisably, just give up, please give up now!
Forgive me for digressions, these words were much ado cerebral digestion.
Circling back to the critical lesson as time draws to an end for this session.

Let us join hand in hand together while we watch Mondays burn forever.
Life will be much better for the human race as we kick them out...to outer space.
*Everybody now!* Waving bye-bye to Mondays, they're not really fun days,
Not so sweet like Sundays
But you know what?
They can kiss my ass.

*Everyone has a unique and beautiful light. It is your job to love yourself. It is your only job to love yourself. To find yourself and share this unique and beautiful light. Big changes happen one light at a time.*

*Hint: You're right here, always.*

# Twinkling Eyes

Oh my, hide your dreams so bright.
Glazed over,
By the world's hurting fright.
Step out now,
Come on, don't be shy.
Do you ever question your own precious life?
We live for that one reason why,
But why?

Twinkling eyes,
No matter the hardest climb,
You'll get there in your own time.
Don't forget to,
Share your smile.
Remember, this ride just lasts a while.
Twinkling Eyes,
Beauty lies in your life.
Look up now while there still is time.
Please set this world afire,
With endless love and light.
In your twinkling eyes.

*Breaking news! Chad and Ashley finished their "romantic" dinner date at the prestigious Olive Garden. The tension between the two is heating up after such a meal. The lovebirds whined (yes, the complaining kind), dined, had an "eh, it was fine" time and ate copious amounts of gluten.*

*WARNING: This song is explicitly dirty.*

*Dear Reader, the time calls to lock the door, light a luxurious "fresh-linen" scented candle and reach for the... toilet paper. Hey, don't say I didn't warn you.*

# Mambo No. Two

Let me set the scene for you...

You're on a cute date with the Boo.
Up until now, right about now,
Everything has been going smoothie smooth.
Until that feeling hits...quickly quickly, quick!
Need to find that restroom.

When you got to go Number Two!

As a girly girl, it's my job to be "cute."
Never, ever throw off a groove.
Behooved to go with the flowing mood.
Still, the feeling cannot be confused.
Wish it was number one...but it doesn't *feel* like "the one."
Feels like number two.
*Ba do do do DO Do.*

We pull up to the restaurant; doors locked.
He pitches the idea, "Let's walk."
Rhetorically ask back, "Hm, why not?"
We walk around to enjoy the view.
Fully aware deep down of the truth...
Movement only moves the stool.

"Be a girly girl, do what girly girls do."
...But you really got to poo.

Now that boy's catching on to you.
My Momma didn't raise no fool!
*Psst! This is what you do.*

Wave it off and say, "Nah, I'm fine, uh—this is just a new dance move."
He looks skeptical at you. *Time to sell the move.*
Sidestep-snap, sidestep-snap.
Sidestep-snap. One, two!

Look, I'm telling you; this is just a new dance move!
He believes you for a moment...
*Oh, phew!*

*Ra da da da DA, A-dee dee dee dee DEE.*
The moral of the story is...Uh...
Everyone in the world, even all the boys and girls,
We all go number two.

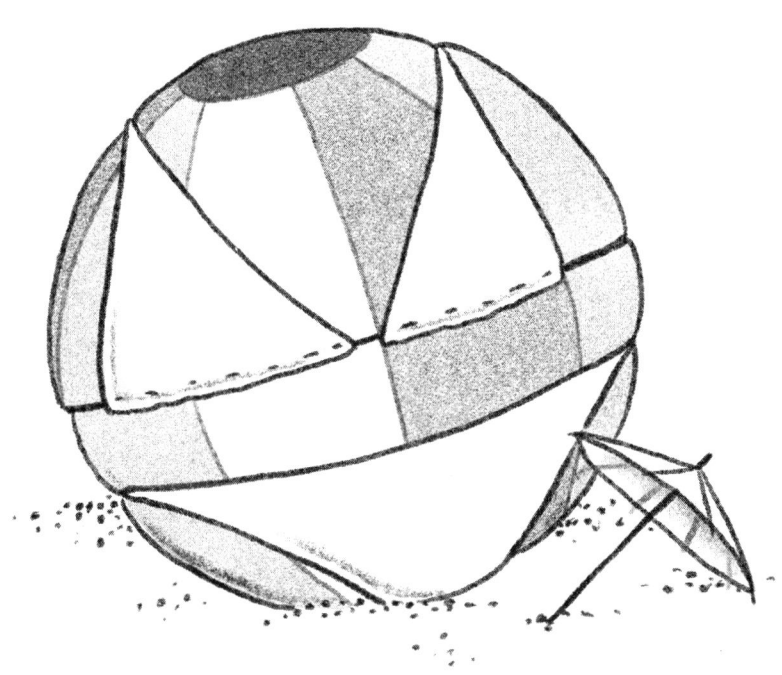

Seasons may change yet extra pounds around the hips remain. May your naughty winter bodies see the light of day regardless.

Sweater weather is all-season weather.

# Summer Blubber

I'm too hot for the summer, so hot in the summer.
Failed to lose the blubber, ate one too many suppers.
My body is now covered but trying again next summer.
Then probably steal your lover, better hide your lover.
'Cause I'm too hot for the summer, so hot in the summer!

Not trying to brag but I'm always the first pick for the volleyball team.
With my chin held high, I'm standing up tall, until they realize…

I'm not a beach volleyball! No…
I'm not a Beach volley—

I'm too hot for the summer, so hot in the summer.
They say, "*Better luck next summer, always another summer!*"

I'm registered as too hot, too hot in the first degree.
90-percent sunburn exactly.
Check out these sweat stains on my sweatshirt,
Tell me what you see.
Like a Rorschach blot test on my back,
Is it a duck or a fuzzy bunny?

You tell me, because I can't see.
*Duh.*

Red face, salty skin.
Sandy, sandy bottoms.
Waist deep, I'm going in.
Bikini wax, no AC.
Oops, I missed a hair—*Ew!*
Sticking to your leather seat. You can't get rid of me—No.

I'll be looking like a model from *Trainwreck* magazine.
Call me Samantha, though better known as *Miss Hot Mess 2019.*
'Cause I'm too hot for the summer,
Too hot in the summer!

Granted, some addictions are better than others. For instance, a gym addiction would be "Goals." What about combining addictions? ...Why am I a Genius? Good question.

Take a "strong passion" for food and another "even stronger passion" for shopping and squish them together. This fitting combo makes the Life game much more fascinating. Merely as an example, not speaking from personal experience or anything silly like that.

# Superstore

Going to the Superstore, super fun and not a chore.
Good times at the Superstore. Made a list but what's it for?
No point to it, not to this list, I never, ever stick to it.

Walking up to the Superstore,
This guy outside tries to sell me popcorn, *popcorn?*
No Sir, no thank you, Sir. I don't want your popcorn.
You see this list? I really ought to stick to it.
Look down double-check, oh shit.
"Popcorn" written on my list although the one I want is different.
*Just keep walking, just keep walking...*
Act like that never happened.

First things first, grab a handy-wipe, hand-wipe.
Give that cart a good handy-job, hand-job.
Wipe away those dirty germs, dirty germs.
I look like a dirty girl, dirty girl.
This girl is virtually, sickness-free.
*No, not me!*

Walking up and down the aisles though this counts as my cardio.
Heart rate in the fat-burning zone, call it kill two birds, one stone.
*Oh, crap!* There is someone I know,
Look at Joe, don't look at Joe. No place to run or hide, *Oh, no!*
It's all too late, eye contact already made.
We begin to say a dumb phrase...

*"Hi, how are you?"* - "Good."
*"How are things?"* - "Good."
*"Well... good to see you."* - "You as well."
Everything is good-good.

Back to shopping, filling up my cart so full.
Racks on stacks on snacks on crafts, scented soap, bubble bath.
Toys for Hammy hamster, praying to remember Item #1: TOILET PAPER.
'Tis a reminder that I'm getting older.

Got to stick to the list, to the list.
I'm a self-check-out bitch, check-out bitch.
While I'm here I should make the most of it,
That way I'll save a trip. *(Lies!)*

Tomorrow I'll be back again, going to the Superstore, the Superstore.
The End.

FYI: *<u>Hoops</u> is a classy sports bar located in Yakima, WA.
FYFI: (For your further information) The word <u>classy</u> can be substituted for <u>trashy</u>.

*Adjectives are relative. You'll soon understand.*
*There once was a white-trash girl,*
*Who danced around and twirled.*
*Every Monday night,*
*Religiously drinking diet vodka Sprite,*
*She drank too much and hurled.*
*Nevertheless, she did not quit,*
*Even more room was left in "little girl's" stomach.*
*Eventually she changed her ways,*
*Looked into the mirror to say, "No more for me!"*
*So, she wrote this song,*
*To embody some of her wrongs.*
*Ladies and Gentlemen, presenting the "Whoopsie Daisy" song.*

# Whoopsie Daisy

Whoo, girl! Whoo-hoo!
We're going out, going out with who?
Just girls, just us girls! So said without, without them boys.
Told myself that I'd stop drinking, really that's some wishful thinking.
Waking up the next day,
With a "raging-thumping-bumping-goodness-gracious-why am I like this?"-
Headache.
Chugging all the Gatorade, as the night comes back in little flashbacks,
Why do I do this anyway?
I promised that I'd change. A new resolution.
Come next week, cringey night repeats, now we're back at *Hoops* again...
*FUCK.*

*Yoo-hoo!* My sweet bartender, the unusual for me.
Something hard but soft, not too much, just enough and of course, BUBBLY!
Whoo! One drink in, feeling a little boozy-loosey-goosey.
Somebody try and whoo me.
*Do...do you feel it? Yeah, I feel it.*

Whoo! Girl, that's my song.
We are screaming it at the top of our lungs. Sounding off-key the whole night
long.
Twerking it but the twerk not strong.
Picture this: Granny Tammy's fanny, moving side-to-side in jammies.

All the boys were gawking,
Or more like, "What the fucking?"

Whoo! Girl, hold my hair,
My hard but soft, not too much, just enough drink is coming up everywhere.
It's still BUBBLY!

Missed the toilet, that's okay, my makeup still looks cute. *Hey hey, don't go into stall #2.*

Walk into the bathroom alone,
Left with six new *Whoo*-girlfriends made in tow.
What a typical Monday night, all the drinks are priced half-price.
Kind of wish I could do it over.

Totally a one well *"oh well"* two-dollar hangover.

Remember the days when you tuned out mother's ol' rhyming catch phrases meant to create "peace" between you and your evil sibling? Me neither. Nevertheless, you obeyed like a good little girl (or boy) so the 3 cookies a day privileges would not be taken away. Me too. These nursery "childhood life principles" hardly made any sense anyways but damn, were they catchy. However, we trust that "Mother knows best" even if her tactics are utter nonsense. This could really explain much of these silly poems. Ah, time to call the therapist...

# Comparing Is Caring

We all have problems, and daddy issues.
Name the heartbreaks, setbacks and felt misused.
No one is alone, sometimes it seems not so.
If you don't believe and need help pronto,
Here's a little dirty cheat sheet.

Compare yourself to others,
Not the most noble thing to do.
Compare yourself to others,
A guaranteed way to lose the blues.
More specifically and accurately compare yourself to those...
Those less fortunate than you!

Volunteer at the shelter,
Serve a meal to Billy-bob Joe!
He doesn't know whether,
The food's talking back to him—"*Oh, no!*"
Pet a dog with three legs,
At least you weren't the one who got pegged.

Comparing makes life bright, or brighter than before.
Get up off your ass, we live in America after all.
Look to your left, look to your right,
There's a reason to be thankful, someone's always worse off at the table.
But if you're alone then you're screwed!

There's nothing much else to lose.
Sinking self-esteem has tanked,
The very easiest way to give thanks.
*Hey, thanks! I feel better!*
Oh, but however, let us consider other ways than the latter.

Throw cash to a shrink, hit the town for too many drinks.
Stop for a moment and think.
Comparing forever saves you time, money, and the liver.
It doesn't sound clever, but I'll say whatever!
Who really cares what is noble to do?
Last time I checked it's not Sunday,
While those guys over there are serving up booze!
It's not good advice, simply my lonely point of view.
As a quick way, a sure way,
To cure your silly blues.
Compare yourself to those...who suck more than you.
*Boo-hoo.*

Let's do some simple mental math here. Add together one 5-hour flight wait, 3 goat cheese salads and one "sort of-kind of" vegan digestion system... what do you get? Stumped? Read more to find out.

Plug your nose and away we go!

# Flying Stinks

I'm going to die on this airplane (*die on this airplane*).
Not in a cool way (*not in a cool way*),
Not a hijack crash and burn,
Or accident from a wrong turn,
Doesn't mean it doesn't hurt.
There's always more than one way to die,
When you're up a mile high.

Someone farted on the airplane (*they farted on the airplane*).
I think I'm going to suffocate (*I'm going to suffocate*).
This is not a death of dignity, plug my nose, refuse to breathe.
Oh my God, what did they eat? *On the airplane!*
Fresh air is a commodity, not found on flight 2-4-2-3.
Why don't these O2 masks release? *On the airplane!*

*Well, if that doesn't do it then…*

I'm still going to die on this airplane.
My ears are in extreme pain.
They hurt from the pressure change,
Plugged up from the pressure change.
Forgot my gum, a grave mistake.
Airport prices? *Yeah, no thanks!*
Who pays eight bucks a pack anyways?

Death is coming for me,
The End ain't looking so pretty.

Picture a guy drooling on my shoulder,
Snoring like a boulder,
Armrests are taken over,

*Where do I put my arms now?*
Toes getting jammed in the aisle,
Elbows stabbing left and right,
To get comfortable is such a fight!

Though there's a secret I can no longer keep,
Because all along the fart came from...

Me.

I ate a salad with GOOOOAAAAT cheese.